Bereavements:

The Selected and Collected Poems

Not always in the present form, these poems have appeared variously in: *Malahat Review, New Letters, Kayak, Quarry, Sewanee, Poetry Northwest, Tar River Poetry, Southwest Review, The Reaper, Cincinnati Review, Interim, Sierra Journal, West Coast Review, Accent, Poetry, Poetry Lore.* "Necessary Encounters" appeared first in *Oregon Signatures*, a centennial volume of Oregon poetry.

Books by James B. Hall:

NOVELS:
Not By the Door
Racers to the Sun
Mayo Sergeant

POETRY:
The Hunt Within
Bereavements: Selected and Collected

SHORT STORY COLLECTIONS:
15 x 3 (with Cassill & Gold)
Us He Devours
The Short Hall
I Like It Better Now

ANTHOLOGIES:
Realm of Fiction (3/e)
Modern Culture & The Arts (with Ulanov)

(And Others)

Bereavements:

The Selected and Collected Poems

by

James B. Hall

<>

Introduction by HAZARD ADAMS

<><> *Story Line Press / Castle Peak Editions* <><>

ISBN: 0-934257-62-0 (cloth)
ISBN: 0-934257-63-9 (paper)

Story Line Press
Three Oaks Farm
Brownsville, Oregon 97327-9718

Castle Peak Editions
P.O. Box 342
Williams, Oregon 97544

Library of Congress Catalog Card Number: 91-72463

For James Laughlin

Table Of Contents

IV: TRANSPORT TO WINTER

V: ADVENTURES IN NARRATION

In for the Long Haul:

an Introduction by HAZARD ADAMS

On page ninety-four of this collection, the poet, in a dream vision reminiscent of Dante and Keats, meets three dead writers—Faulkner, Dreiser, and Stevens. They query him on the state of writing in America. After preliminaries, he answers concerning

> The writer's way inside
>
> Our capitalistic system:
> Those taken in the scramble
> For money, dissolved by drink,
>
> Friends who bartered
> Talent for the symphonic
> Illusions of drugs, or the honey
>
> Of protest. Others fell
> Into a jackal-agent's bed
> Or for quick fame, now,
>
> Became personalities of straw,
> Could very well imitate
> Themselves, or feed the presses.

This report from our world is not made by way of apology for the writer in a capitalistic system. In the poet's view, it seems, these writers succumbed, were not strong enough to go it alone over the long haul.

To none of the ills, all terminal, has James B. Hall allowed himself to become victim, and this collection attests to that. Though a distinguished leader of writing programs at Oregon, Irvine, and Santa Cruz, he has never "revise[d] for tenure, / fringe benefits aforethought" (100). Indeed, he has always been deliberately something of an outsider among writers. At the end of the poem from which I have quoted, the shades of Faulkner, Dreiser, and Stevens enlarge themselves beyond bound; and when they disappear (not by diminishment but by sublime greatness), the poet declares himself to feel "more alone / Than ever I remembered." I think Hall has always put, or at least grown to put, family first, a vision of the writer's vocation strongly second, and everything else after that. Hall was born with or early acquired a love of language and of fictions. In a fairly lengthy autobiographical statement written for *Contemporary Authors,* which takes his life up to acceptance for publication of his first story, he tells of establishing early the habit of eating crackers and reading in bed late into the early morning. He read "for the action, the heraldry, and 'the way it came out'." He developed also a sure ear for voices and an appreciation of the real rhetoric of farms and small towns. In his short stories and his poems that low mimetic rhetoric is mixed with high mimetic gesture. For years it has produced unique results in Hall's short stories, even in those where the character is fantastic in a real world (I think of "The Freezer Bandit") or real in a fantastic one ("My Work in California"). In the poems the result is striking, as in the bitter words of Hall's coyote:

> Oh on
> That day I shall command these hills
> To convulse, to send out packs not yet dreamed
> By grocery shoppers. (89)

This is a coyote who almost quotes from *Hamlet*, but is truly animal. Hall has written of his childhood:

> At that time farm life in Ohio is conventionally thought to be the hayseed life, pastoral, early to bed, etc., etc.
>
> In fact our house was high-talk, musical, free-wheeling, highly emotional, fully argumentative, and possibly Bohemian.

The combination of low and high talk, of a deliberate play of linguistic wit (as in the word "possibly" above), and a certain formality and distance verging on the *noli me tangere* sort is, as he remarked recently in a letter, "not well received by the Plain Speakers. I am all with Marlowe and the mighty line, no doubt":

> These things lay down beside roomettes,
> Turbo-sex with chilled white wine. . .
> These things, these things lay down. (84)

Or, from the marvelous poem "Bereavements":

> But most often at home
> When our five children
> Talk or are all reading
> Together, Oh, I miss them
> So, and for one moment
> Silently, I show myself. (80)

The combination comes, I think (I had an Ohio farm father), from Hall's thorough grasp and assimilation of the speech and attitude of wit of the Ohio farm and small-town world of his youth:

Lord, we are your honest farmers
And — in all good order — our Books:
Note the long, bad years of your own tornadoes
Yet we rebuild granary roofs in due season. (30)

and

And as for money
I know the true-stroked ball rolls
True, and Brother, I say if you
Play long enough with me, you lose. (91)

The autobiographical statement I have quoted from takes Hall's life through his early years and those of World War II. For his poems, these were very important times. They provided much of his subject matter and, I think, almost all the perspective and tone. It is a perspective and tone matured and honed in language over a subsequent academic career in which Hall's ideal and perhaps imagined hero was the man of letters. A product of the University of Iowa's Writers' Workshop in its immediate post-war days—its perhaps "heroic phase," as Hall has called it—he also received the doctorate from Iowa. Not a "specialist," as are so many writers (and scholars) today, he has published novels, short story collections, and poems. He has edited anthologies, to which he has contributed practical criticism. He has encouraged students to *write*.

In "Our Masters, Revisited," from which I quoted at the beginning, the poet discovers that the three dead writers inhabit an eternity in which are provided a good desk and a panoramic view:

Each day in this lucid
Place they revised forever
Those things they loved best. (95)

They are pleased to be spending eternity in this way. Hall is himself an indefatigable reviser, and, I suspect, would be an eternal one. In his first and only previous collection of poems (*The Hunt Within*, 1973) there were thirty poems altogether. He has deleted ten of these from the "*Selected* and Collected Poems" [my italics] and has revised almost all of the twenty that have survived, some quite substantially. An impressive example is "A Tenant Foresees Payment Due," originally entitled simply "The Tenant." It is really a totally new poem, no line having escaped thorough rewriting. The poem is enlarged from four to five stanzas, yet its number of lines is decreased from thirty-six to thirty.

Some revisers are deleters, some work by accretion. It is interesting to observe what Hall does with the early "My Father" (33), a poem that I am sure means much to him. The changes are unerringly toward precision, the exchange of a word or phrase, and deletion of the unnecessarily decorative modifier. "Antique snow" (l. 5) becomes simply "old snow." This snow "Of memory falls adrift upon his days" (l. 6), whereas in the first version it had fallen "across his heart." A "green room" becomes a "hot room." A "vast black wink of night" gains specificity (l. 36) with "long black wink." A "that" is replaced by "this" to gain immediacy and specify the point of view. The conclusion is made tighter and introduces a new hint of characterization, motivation, and attitude. Early version:

> Instead he thinks upon
> A crossroad, a wreck, and a daughter, dead,
> And of his son who sometimes ships a box of pears
> From Oregon or towards midnight may telephone, collect.

The last line is changed to:

> From Oregon, or is curious, telephones collect.

A whole stanza and a definite article disappear from "In Bailey Woods." The title poem of the first volume, "The Hunt Within," deletes two stanzas and numerous other words. We may have here an Ohio farm boy's parsimony at work; it's also, and foremost, a faithful and patient attention to craft. Hall has written to me, "I tend not to write a great many poems each year, but I work them over, and over; I dislike the open-mike school of verse, for they are too often only topical."

The poems selected and collected here are not arranged chronologically by time of composition. Given Hall's method of continual revision, that would be impossible. Nor can we presume arrangement by autobiography, fictive or otherwise. Clearly, Hall does not want them read in either of these topical ways. There is, however, a general thematic arrangement by groups, and to some extent they provide the artistic illusion of a life, though one to which a deliberate twist is given; we see that Hall's elegy for himself and other poems of loss and death do not conclude the volume. They remain prophetic; there is more work to be done and, without a doubt, more revision. Another section of poems follows.

I shall return to this, but it is first worthwhile to consider briefly the four sections that precede the concluding one. "In the Country" and "In the Towns" are Hall's innocence and experience. Some of William Blake's innocence poems have the bite of experience. All of Hall's do. They are, when about youth, remembrances of it; when not they recall adult figures from youth and family. Hall's country and town poems do not paint a pastoral scene and then a scene of decadent sophistication. In the first place, these are towns, not cities; and in the second, Hall doesn't write about country and town as such but almost always about people. And anyway, town and country are not far apart in Ohio, or Oregon, for that matter. Seven of the nine poems of "In the Country" are early, three of the eight of "In the Towns." In the latter the special Hall voice is particularly apparent. It produces the odd angle of vision, the occasional surrealism, the first of Hall's emblematic animals (the giraffe), dramatic monologues from the dead, and instruction in what to do with the deer you have hunted and killed, the last infused with that certain Hallian outsideness, as if we are to make some decision.

The third section, "Patrols," is pivotal and contains some of Hall's most powerful earlier work. Here there is identification by an oblique sympathy with previous writers all the way back to Old English poets, explicitly with Trakl and Mandelstam, and, by deliberate emulation in "Memorial Day, 1959," of two poems ("In Memory of Major Robert Gregory" and "Easter, 1916"), with Yeats. There are others recalled by a word or phrase: Dylan Thomas, Wallace Stevens, W. H. Auden. There is also a dramatic monologue that competes with Browning ("In the Compounds of Error," this, however, in Part V). I think that Hall learned some things from Robert Penn Warren and Robert Lowell. These hints and emulations of others have mainly dramatic motives. The whole section "Patrols" is composed of midlife poems about actions. The patrols are patrols of violence, of war, and in one poem the dangers of love and association. In "Love's Terrain," the ground here that Hall patrols is love, the addressee is a beloved, the symbolic world voyaged through a cavern, a cool inferno of the speaker's past deeds. Then there is a movement downward into water and finally a cliff's ledge, where

> We discover only the mercy of granite, a lantern
> Filled with snow, a fissure's awful reconciliation.
> These things I show you honestly before we kiss. (63)

Among these poems lurk the dragon Volant and Dick's mate, Moby Jane, both with their stories, told in the voice of the Other, for which it is Hall's ability so cunningly to find the right cadence and diction. Hall's Volant is no likeable, friendly, sentimental dragon but one deserving our respect and fear for being essentially animal. Moby Dick, his wife reports with a certain wifely knowledge, was at his end as crazed as Ahab, though Ahab's opposite, practicing one world and love to "sea lions at rut" while men hunt them with clubs.

There is enough death in "Patrols" to make the movement to "Transport to Winter" no surprise. All of the poems here have been written since his first book of poetry, *The Hunt Within*. They move toward the powerful "Bereavements" and those poems of finality that follow. The section title is a response, friendly but by stark opposition, to Stevens' "Transport to Summer" and to the deliberate gaudiness of his "Auroras of Autumn." They have a certain straightforwardness of movement leading to summary statement.

But then there is an adventure, specifically the final section "Adventures in Narration." The traditional Platonic and Aristotelean distinction between narration and imitation (mimesis) is that in the former there is a single narrator who *tells* us the story, as Homer does, and in the latter there are people who speak as on a stage. Hall's narrations are always mimetic, which is to say they are dramatic, even though the narrators may be performing only on the stage of themselves. They always have a specific voice, and frequently they exhibit a sort of verbal exuberance or playing to their audience that they may not understand themselves, being so clearly *themselves*: yet the voice is by empathy always clearly Hall's voice. I would like to characterize it as the true voice of fiction. This voice is one that would arrange the facts to achieve the effect, mold the case for the sake of an heroic "untruth," narrator and author both guilty. Anyone who has read Hall's fiction has had experience of this voice in, for example, "The Freezer Bandit" or the fantastic stories in *The Short Hall*, but also the realistic ones.

There is a classical and medieval tradition dominated by philosophers and theologians accusing the poet of lying. Four centuries ago, Sir Philip Sidney tried to lay it to rest with the claim that the question of truth or lie was irrelevant to fiction. There will always be something about the poem that tempts the suspicion of those who want a certain *truth* and are disturbed by *voice* with its deliberate feigning disregard. It is best characterized here by the production of a certain voice speaking with another certain voice, both banishable from Plato's *Republic*. (Hall actually dramatizes the fear of the possible absence of one's *own* voice in "Elegy, My Own" in a way that echoes Plato's suspicion of the feigning poet.) The Hall voice of Judas:

> They are saying I hanged myself?
> Well, sit down — have a sherbet. (99)

Of Saint John:

> His great appeal?
> Why, I should say the Master
> Exploited practicality. (103)

The animals of the ark:

> We give
> Noah and all management, less than a week. (104)

The dog:

> I say if dogs had hands for paws
> We'd soon see who barked in pens. (87)

My stooping to Arnoldian (well, no) touchstones here is a sincere form of flattery, this critic unable to formulate an adequate description for these marvelous effects. The ventriloquist is always present even as the speaking voice is unique. There has been, I suspect, something disconcerting to some readers and, I am sure, publishers in the obliquity of Hall's artistry. Certainly some have thought: If I play with this Jack long enough, I will indeed lose. I certainly hope so.

Bereavements:

The Selected and Collected

Poems

I.

In The Country

At Skulk, the Young Vandal

Long past my time for bed,
More quiet than any bone,
Often that spring I lay outstretched
Between forsythia and the limestone
Foundation of the Midland M. E. Church;

Not once seen from the street, alone,
I waited for all cars to pass
And overhead between Elm-tree forks
Saw the tombstone walls and steeple
Float on the moonlight's enormous breath.

Then branch upward by maple branch
I became a shadow swinging
To the vestry roof, walked the ridgecap,
Paused beside the mouth of a carved, damp cornice,
Slid like a lizard into their belfry.

Among the dark, peaked, dormant rafters overhead,
Feathers fouled the last-year's pigeon nests,
But I stood between two iron shadows
Of two iron Methodist bells, laughed
At trees dreaming in the blue streets below.

Down through the hiss of cobwebs,
Down through a waterfall of dust
Where bats at roost trembled, mewed,
I saw a million sparrow turds turn
Mauve in a stained-glass window's glow;

The cold, curved, square duct of tin
Took me crawling to a choir-loft grille
Until, headfirst but not born again,
I came out into the waist-deep odor
Of varnish, the hymnal murmur of pews.

Their basement in moonlight was a white sand
Beach, used mostly to store things for children:
Six fish in a fish bowl's slime;
Clay for modeling; an angel-doll in a cradle;
A freezer, austere, in its own white enamel.

II.

Often that summer I went there,
Viewed my own death — by falling — on flagstones
Or in rainstorms lolled high in their steeple
To watch the long, green typhoon heave
Of hayfields, there plotted my flight to the sea.

Mostly I entered to look for dropped money,
Was foraging, was stretched beneath pews
When the latch of the great Methodist door
Rattled, then slowly, honestly, opened . . .
And suddenly, in the aisle, I saw two shoes.

Trapped, mouth pressed to the sisal
Rug, I watched two feet and her purse
Hesitate, and then a woman all at once
Sat down, then sighed, almost above my head
So close I might have touched her hem.

Instead, motionless, the two of us so near
And yet alone in the stained-glass shadows
Of the M.E. church, I overheard her prayers.
For Elwood, so often away to work for the B & O:
Please, sleep safe this night in Chillicothe;

For mother: please cure her cancer soon in heaven;
For her two children: their boils to heal, and please,
Their bedtime quarrels to cease when he's away;
Also: give help tomorrow to all home canners.
These things only for others, and nothing more.

Then someone's wife I could not see
Stood devoutly for one minute in the aisle,
Turned slowly back towards the vestry doors,
Looked into that dark, Ohio street,
Paused, then stepped down, went home.

By proverb, by cunning, very well I knew
Where there's one, there's two so I laid
Low — but breathed a little — counted ten,
Then swaggered past the umbrella racks,
Found my bike still parked beneath the shrubbery.

Frightened at last, furiously I pedaled
The cemetery path headlong through a hedge
Until sidewalks rolled hot beneath my wheels
Headed for all-night railroad restaurants
Where dimes and my illicit missionary quarters

Went for gum, for cigarettes — no questions asked;
Or, for side-bets always on the field in crap games
Floating through a dozen pool room toilets;
Or, to the bar room of the Silver Barn,
Where for a dime Piano-John played, "Roll 'em Pete."

Oh, in that way I came to know church doors
May not be locked at night, but never again
Walked on all-fours across the ridgecap,
Rode the storm-high steeple in thunder nor saw
Fireballs roll for miles along the power lines.

Yet, years later, braced on the bridgewing
Of a freighter, deck plates sprung beyond all land's end,
When neither word nor bell stays the sea's final
Consummation, on every watch of each raging day
Of my life, I sought the thing I thought I fled.

In Bailey Woods

Oh young my farmer
Blood and nine, so I leaped
To hear our dogs break our barnyard
Kennels, the limping fox crouched in their eyes,
And Redbone's nostril eager for split entrails
In Bailey's woods;

Then mother, goodbye:
For somewhere in our swamps
A bitch-fox waits in her hollow log
While dogs lope through the scrub oak grove,
Answering the horn's throat, the following call,
Through Bailey woods.

And there in trees
Old Redbone bayed his hunter's
Heart away, then fell. The fox
Circled, circled, circled our night, trailed
Our pack, back-tracked into a reach of Sandy Creek
And there through briars

Watched our dogs
Sink flank-deep in Long-Time Slough,
Their legs taking the sand-bars of that
Creek, until they shook mud in spangles
From their backs, lost her trail
In Bailey woods.

Therefore much I
Hunted on patrols beyond barbed
Wire into my own Alsatian nights
Where a flare, slipped by a Very pistol
Cleaned night away, and a corporal found his winter
In some other woods;

But I am nine
And fifty, now, could wish to hear
A hound's bones bay across a swamp,
To take away these burnt-out timber lands
For this night's pack and swamp are one
In Bailey woods.

The Hunt Within

That hill
Is humped, raising its weight
Of snow towards the sun
That burns away the high fog, a dawn
Of a new mid-winter

And the scrub pine
Bristles on that hill's back
Like hackles while my hound
Digs memory's root of a fox dead,
A bone forgotten.

Now the picket
Crow calls black, clarion news
Beyond these indifferent woods
And the last berry of summer
Drops without a sound

While my dog
Grovels the hillock's bluest snow
Whimpering from his forepaw's
Slit tenderness. Now my gun's
Full-primed,

Eager shells
Ram home to their steel chamber,
And I want to see
A man crouched, or better, running,
And shoot him dead,

Like any game.
Therefore I hunt beneath sumacs
On the dirty little footprints
Of revenge, maim even the snipe's
Contorted wings,

Explode a squirrel's
Grey brief chattering hide,
For vengeance on this land
Burns, bloody, burns firm beneath

My hunting jacket,
To take revenge
Against this land which made me.
My hound claws
The entrails of the hill, the briar whipping
Fires my eye

And the tear
From the thorn or the wind only
Takes its course among these hackles
On my cheek, snuffs, answers the ancient
Baying dog within.

Grandmother

Calls now for husband
But he no more drops
The hames or a bent coupling pin
To answer the voice of her cane
Thumping across the porch floor to fetch him;

Calls now for her dinner
But cannot remember
How just now her porridge steamed
While the old growl inside her
Sucked spoon, then gnawed the bowl.

She rocks upon the sills
Of her past anger, powerless
While the weed patch of her brain
Blossoms again with memories of a small
Livery stable near the depot
And how in the rain

He drove the small bay
Gelding out at midnight to cart
Those trollop nuns to St. Martin's,
And how near daylight she lashed him into straw
With a buggy whip, let blood later,
With her jealous tongue.

Stares across
Her old Sunday lawns of memory
Into the autumn fields which lay
Wrinkled, shrunk, like bee-stung plums;
Sees there her own decaying face
A gully only of senile clay.

Yet turns to business,
And while hills doze in this sun
Like simpletons she thumps for tea,
And with the cunning of the very old
Shows all her sly, antique buttons
She has bequeathed to me.

Pilgrims: Uncle Sid

In water is recognition
And therefore my Uncle Sid
Stared something less than forty years
Into a falling, or a rising, reservoir.

When the B & O dammed up a reach
Of Honey Creek they took him on,
When young, to lower or to raise
Their floodgates, according to season;

And so my Uncle Sid arose
And walked out each winter day
Six miles to work and then walked back:
A watcher of water, and sometimes small carp.

But good only as a watcher
Of water, it was well said,
For in the droughts of summer
He slept upright on an old nail keg;

And, being twice bought, he elected
Not to fish, or vote, or even speak
Until at last it was well said
That he, himself, was much like water.

After something less than forty years
He died one night, in his house,
In his own bed, grim to the very end
When his own sluice gates sprung

Inside the reaches of his lungs,
Uncaged that vast calamity of waters
Which cleansed not much at all from his wallet
Then flooded forever the mud flats of his brain.

The Field Hand's Dream

At noon these
Fence rows doze in the comprehensive
Blue of summer and all berries
Fall to the simple justice
of worms.

By these signs,
And a thousand other hooded
Ways, God shuttles His working hand
And therefore even devout prophecies
of flood,

Shortfall of water,
A stallion's sullen withdrawal from mares,
Or the outrageous appetite of locusts —
These temporalities give way to Providence —
Towards evening;

Or, past midnight,
Adrift on the foxfire monody of dreams
I float with the quail's whistle
Among willows, embrace clover growing,
And often see

The hay fork's
Untracked, glistening tines scythe
Down from the darkness of barns to become
Light, pinned rustling to this season's
Azure flowers.

Whereupon I do
Awake in the stalk-time of frost,
Feel the hames, the weather of my years
Go slack against the moonlit
Drifts of winter.

Then I recollect
Those old wings used once, stored
Wet in a closet, their webs cracked,
The buckles of brass tarnished
By unregenerate mold.

Ohio Farmers, at Resurrection

Lord, we are your honest farmers
And — all in good order — our Books:

Note the long, bad years of your own tornadoes
Yet we rebuilt granary roofs in due season;

Note other Expense against Accounts Receivable,
Their outrageous charges for hauling, paid in kind.

We mention also about twenty shoats shamefully taken
By cholera — no doubt *all* according to your plan?

Yet, we are your farmers regardless of season
And therefore we, ourselves, claim some improvements.

Furthermore, Sir, we sold short all your Winter wheat
Thus turned good judgment into capital gains.

Truly Lord, we are your absolutely honest farmers
But be forewarned of all their stockyard rumors:

The nice husbandry of two sets of ledgers,
Or alfalfa sold, then charged off to drought;

Those malignant tales were hatched in the weevil
Throats of merchants, all Brothers of the Golden Thumb.

Against calumny, Sir, we place this paid-for church,
Your pews at hymn — and all built with ample parking.

Reason enough, before you do this Day's Glorious
Work, to state our one well-considered proposition:

Forever we shall accept the depreciation of barns,
Upkeep on all line-fences, the sicklebacked weasel

Among pullets, and the distemper of Your certain droughts;
Yes, and all unforeseen calamities, merely for your
dispensation

For us to mow our clover, so near fruition
And also to hold — only for our children — title to all land

Until, in your own time You do return, as now,
And do assume forever the direct management

Of these unregenerate woods, this cut-over land
Which as we watch You will transmute to gold.

Then even from a squall line across the winter sky —
Which is your hand opening — we shall see larks rise:
Consider this thing well, Lord, for we are your Honest
Farmers.

A Tenant Foresees Payment Due

Inside your woods,
The terrain again familiar,
I squat beside your leaf-shaped
Pool, stare at my own face
And my billed cap held
Among ferns at the water's edge.

Past midnight the hedgehog
Drinks. Past noon the sun
Warps clouds across the sky.
Held so in this intemperate water,
I eat acorns, see delirium in moss,
Become the sheet lightning of dreams.

My shotgun rusted at half-cock,
Towards dusk at first snowfall
I depart the stumps, the cutover days
Of Indian Summer. Yet I saw a vast
Grey squirrel float among branches
And also frost caught in barbwire moonlight.

Once again at home to wife,
I manage the dark catalepsy
Of barns, the equity of stanchions,
The weevil's revenge on innocent wheat;
Now I endure all things made of sleet,
The wet hides of cold days dying.

The foreclosure of winter is at hand
And even the shadows of mice will freeze.
Landlords, asleep in afternoon towns,
I tell you these things honestly,
I who each spring travel there
See shoats, see babies among treetops burning.

My Father

In Florida the occult cry of birds
Swings like a net above the trailer parks
Where men talk weather, and stare,
And horseshoes, spinning, score the hours.
Yet, even in Florida, the old snow
Of memory falls adrift upon his days.

Even as my father smells the thunder
Of sunshine across his old Ohio furrows
Where his earth-tramper Percherons
Drove plowshares through a killdeer's nest,
Where, in later years, his Fordson
Tractors shook the roots of every woods.

Oh, he was right among his barns:
To all weevils, subtle in wheat, the gas;
To fence-rooter shoats, the ring;
To clay land, clover; to a swamp more lime;
To women, right tools, and to all men
Who worked, food enough at noon.

Each evening, four nights a week, to town:
Genial in pool room or at a church bazaar
He flexed credit like a flail for his good word
Was gold, and the rummy deck leaped lightly
In his hand until as Master-All-Worshipful,
He made Tau his lodge doors against the world.

But now sits in Florida where orange
Trees grow skyward under a reeking sun
And the gaping, bright-gilled tourists
Feed on the palm tree's habit-forming shade —
Yet from the throat of every gold hibiscus
He hears a cut-shoat's gelded scream.

Of course he knows this mindless sun
Is only show, and he knows the squirming

Everglades must sometime invade his hot,
Mismanaged rooms. But in his customary way
Rolls once and with his face near the wall
Accepts by sleep the long black wink of night.

In this resinous dark, his heart drives
The old catastrophe of blood through veins,
But does not dream. Instead he thinks upon
A crossroad, a wreck, and a daughter, dead,
And of his son who sometimes ships a box of pears
From Oregon, or is curious, telephones collect.

Neccessary Encounters

I. Tortoise

Where hired men bent their backs
Along barbed wire
Across my father's partial soil
A tortoise it was
Old Lee pried from our fence row,
That blue-vine meridian.

A tortoise at noon in the sun's
Shell, dated by carving,
Handed me there in the barbed
Wire fences of the sun,
A March-day of tenants moving
As our line fences heaved
Beneath the flanks of another spring.

A tortoise in hand before I knew
Only a tortoise shell
Held two farms and the high sullen
Dollar of the sun upon its back,
Dated by carving, yet dimly read
In our sun-fenced rows
To a boy's winking, reptile heart.

II. Snake

Where a briar's rough caress
Begat indignant berries
For our casual harvest,
Where a white-oak stump
Burned in its slow fire
Of moss, I saw her;

In the center of our woods
Where lecher briars
Coupled with sumac,
Draping her folds of purple
Scaled-copper against the sky,
Molten, gorged, she slept.

Neither root nor hardpan shuddered
When her slow head
Swayed lewd among leaves

And her sly round reptile eye
Opened, but could not wink
Into the shadows of my trespass;

All art forgotten, she bestirred
Her slattern's flesh,
Roiled across the sumac leaves,
Sought some deeper core of briar
To tell her slack mate
Of guile, seen lately in a boy's eye.

III. Birds

Lapwing, the deceiver
Or the sneaking jay
A martin, purple
As muscadine
On our twittering vines,
Or a horse-turd sparrow
Wallowing the eye of God;

Peewee, the rain prophet,
Or the foraging crow,
The quail, harried by the sun,
Or the swallows at nest
Beshitting our barns;

Shikepoke, crane,
Or pigeons suspended
In that Ohio, pagan air:
Each beak pecked its share
And all worms squealed
Beneath sod or locust bark,
Courted the fury of all meadow larks.

IV. Boy (encounters self)

Barbed wire rusts
In a tortoise sun
Beak by briar may be undone;
What a boy needs know
Need be learned again:
That winter makes snow,
And spring brings rain.

II.

In The Towns

Nine Bright Ideas for Spring

1. Plant a Small Herb Garden

Start thyme, basil, and sage
Each in a sunny pot
And reserve some space
For a Junior Herb Garden:
All little girls will love you for it.

2. Visit Our State Capitol

First, write for an appointment
With your Senior Senator;
And remember to order passes
For the House Visitor's Gallery:
All little boys will love you for it.

3. Go on a Dandelion Hunt

Treat kids to an old-time outing,
Make their greens into a springy salad;
Wash all leaves in luke-warm water,
Toss until everything wilts slightly,
All small worms will love you for it.

4. Build a Simple Birdbath

Surround some water with rocks
(as shown in the above illustration)
But avoid shrubbery or trees
That might hide naughty cats:
Certain sparrows will love you for it.

5. Erect Windowsill Flagpoles

First obtain two smallish flags
From almost any automobile supply store —
Or two kits may be even better:
Bracket, gromets, rope, pulley-wheel. Install.
Patriots in Florida will love you for it.

6. Get Acquainted with the Stars

Spring nights give us constellations
But best use a simple star chart and pointer;
First locate the real Big Dipper,
Then read them the myth of Orion the Hunter.
Astronomers, nationwide, will love you for it.

7. Adopt an Artist

Rembrandt, Wyeth, Mary Cassatt,
Read everything you can about them;
Then buy a few reproductions and don't be
Surprised if all Art *seems much closer.*
If alive, Van Gogh would love you for it.

8. Attend Religious Services of Another Faith

The ecumenical view begins at home,
So build better understanding
    Among all church goers;
Little girls should prepare to cover
Their heads if their thoughts are Episcopalian
    Or even Roman Catholic.
The preachers in Heaven will love you for it.

9. Finally, Make May Baskets

Some rainy afternoon revive
This ancient custom: tell everyone
To place them on the doors of neighbors;
Yes, even on the doors of neighbors
Who say he never will come back
To this large, almost paid-for house.
Someday, almost for sure, almost forever
Little girls will love you for it.

Registered Voters

With his fireaxe all ablaze
The Fireman cut off four toes
Of his good accelerator foot;
His wife wrapped them well in foil,
Four curled-up trout for their freezer.

With his meat scales all askew
At closing time the Butcher smiled
And then cut off his own two ears;
His wife, who mostly took in money,
Tucked them neatly rolled among their sausage.

That night within the judge's chamber,
The Lawyer hummed and with a closing balance
Of an estate cut out the root of his own tongue;
Whereupon his wife buried it still
Pleading beneath the sand of their gas meter.

Now in our Courthouse Square each noon
We see four toes, two ears, and a tongue
At countermarch in brass and old Masonic hats:
They sing, salute, and fire their guns
For better pensions and our four freedoms.

Notes from Baker Street

In trauma of this order the hibiscus
Is always suspect, especially
When blood conflates a tea bag.

Momentarily, in the white cottage,
I shall inspect all calendar dates,
Themselves tainted by eminent domain.

Whereupon, consider the situation
Near Brussels:

> Moskowitz did encounter the pig,
> the dissecting knife, the bacon;
>
> Cromack, the Amsterdam counterfeiter,
> did envy his printer's white canary.
>
> Why, therefore, do the Gravensteins
> tremble before an adagio of candy wrappers
>
> While Mrs. Pogue unravels her anaconda?
> Those things all feign assignation.

Conversely, may not we assume the shears
Is "doing" the Bass Viol, and the repose
Of this sofa truly reveals a guilty party:

Yes, those chairs are a long, innocent row,
Yet detest the backside of life,
And in fact straddle distant snowfields of light.

Watson, surely by now you perceive
The correct tartan of my methods?

My Giraffe: the Whole Story

Not because I was bored
Or because our city planners
Snore at their drafting boards,
And not because I hate the young
At masquerade in leather beards
Nor was it the mushroom-compost
Odor of fatigue from "mobile" homes
Or even because at dusk on Church Street
I paused a long time to stare
Into a mortuary parking lot
Where I heard something, a voice
Calling my real name.

No, most likely I sensed that fame
In Santa Cruz is out of the question
Because if you are not stained-glass
Or artichokes, better to forget it;
Besides convert-vegetarians each day
Stalk the health-food bins, smile,
Are gently superior, but I know
It's trouble later in their lower colons.
Exactly that's what I'm saying now:
Why I brought my nice Giraffe to Santa Cruz.
First, sequin booties personally crocheted
To decorate his two fur-covered horns;
Then a purple-trimmed, all-velvet robe
With two hundred bottle caps for decoration.
Came our first real day of sunshine,
That Giraffe and I on a white-nylon
Tether, we passed *not noticed* into
The Men's Room of our *Daily Sentinel* (newspaper).
From there it was a Giraffe's head swinging
Right on into the Big Man's office (owner)
Me, with the biggest news for Santa Cruz since . . .
"And what," the Big Man said, and sniffed,
"What, Sir, can in fact, I do for you?"

That's exactly when one Giraffe and I —
Nylon tether and all — hit the streets:
Down a parking ramp to Cooper House,
Then to lingerie at Leask's Department Store.
Yet when I led him, sequins and robe sparkling,

Through a low, reechoing arcade to Long's,
Two stoned, flute-playing, happy beggars
Didn't look: they kept right on tuning up, up.
And to be real absolutely honest we got
That same stoned reaction at County Bank —
Also Great Western — for no one *noticed*
One high-art, short-tailed, genuine Giraffe's
Head floating through tree tops along our mall.

That's exactly what I'm saying now:
They only sniffed, and said "Have a good one."
Well, for one week one nice Giraffe
And I really tried to make our contribution
To a better way of life in Santa Cruz —
And then it rained, and I gave up.
Except, brothers, I will say this:
Premature retirement is not so very easy.
First, I carried on a long Giraffe-Rights
Discussion with my V.A. Doctor (also others)
And not one single person was — like now —
Remotely into taking over one very good Giraffe.

Maybe my whole life will always end
Like that: no luck at all in the want ads
Until at night we had to run down an alley
So met this widow whose old garage was vacant.
My advice is very frankly this: try it once,
One-each-day a bushel of "found" artichokes,
Straw, and almost every Friday night
A garage loft, groin-deep in new Giraffe manure.

In
Consequence
Each and every day
Thereafter
My
G
i
r
a
f
f
e
G
o
t
Smaller and smaller
Until (this is sad)
I carried him everywhere
Yes, carried that nice
Warm thing inside my nice-
est inside, velvet-lined
P
o
c
ket:
To Perko's, to All-Nite Drive
Inns, or stopped in shrubbery
To see a lot more than you think
Inside all your bedroom windows
And (when with widow) she paid
For three to view quite a few
X   T
/   h
R   r
a   o
t   a
e   t
d   e
D   d
e   M
e   o
pest   vies.

That's exactly what I'm saying now:
One Giraffe, and how this thing came out.

Which, as was implied above (see picture)
Was this: one nice Giraffe got smaller —
And smaller — until each day it seemed to me
I had nothing left except being more and more
Out of work, until late one night I cried
And cried and finally said to this friend (widow):
"Santa Cruz, go out and find yourself a new one."

And that's when she said, "Doctor, suit yourself,"
Even for our Friday nights said, "Oh, not yet."
So bottle caps, nylon-white tether and all
Just exactly like I'm saying now, I ate it.

Except, to be very frank, I feel no better.
Yet, speaking personally, at all hours
Now I *know* where my nice little thing is.
My tiny little, exactly button-size Giraffe
Is chomping, is swaying his head, is grazing
Right *here*, in the pit of my stomach.

Dressing Your Deer

The season opened at dawn
    and you just killed your first deer.

First, cut its throat crosswise
    to sever the jugular vein;
If, however, your deer's blood is not circulating
    this will not be necessary.

Now:
    through the skin,
    but not into the body cavity,
    between hams and base of the throat,
    make your next incision
        (at this point the brisket
        is very handily opened
        by either a saw or an axe)
    for this allows the windpipe,
        esophagus,
            lungs,
                and
                    heart
    to be removed very readily.

Next:
    while you cut through
    muscle and tissues
    into the body cavity
    observe the diaphragm —
    the thing which separates
    heart and lungs
    from the stomach of your deer.
    Cut this diaphragm muscle
    very carefully
    and completely around
    your deer's body cavity.
    Only now are you ready
    to remove the entire viscera.

All ready?
    Begin
        with the windpipe
    and then
        the esophagus,
            lungs
                liver
                    heart
                        stomach
                            intestines.
    (Keep the liver and heart
    clean: of this, more later.)

In addition:
    we have the problem
    of the bladder and colon:
    now I've always thought
    this was best accomplished
    by either a saw or an axe,
    but be careful: break the bladder
    and you spoil the hams
    for they will taste strong.

A minor point:
    remove any tissues
    spoiled by your shot.

Now skin your deer:
    hang by the head
    then make incisions
        down
            the inside
            of the front
            and of the hind
                legs.

In conclusion:
    your deer can now be quartered
    and hung each night in the fresh air
    or placed in fly-proof bags in the daytime.

One final thing:
    about that liver and heart
    you were careful to keep *clean*.
    Always take these things home,

cut the liver into medium-sized strips,
and inspect for larvae, flukes, and so on.

Toward evening, in your back yard,
light up your charcoal grille
and add a few green twigs
to send up much smoke.

Then call in all
your neighborhood boys
and see how they like to eat
the clean heart and the clean liver
especially when served almost raw.

As for explanations —
should anyone bother to ask —
tell them this:

God put all creatures
on this earth
for our right use.

Bad Habits; Or, Scoring Sunshine

Morning, and my brown ape clucks
In the foliage beside my window,
Shucks his first nut, remains concealed;

Noon, and the mauve light among the trunks
Of pepper trees remains unfractioned, still;
In my kitchen food moults in the cupboard.

Soon night brings the subtle delirium
Of wings and toward morning a hideous
Beak feeds slowly on the zoo-straw of my brain;

From my back porch, at ten o'clock,
I see a fowl suspended among pepper trees,
One eye inspecting its genitals for lice.

Adrift in aqueous, unreconstructed light,
At last I see my ape and the bird touch,
Grotesquely dance — and then they come for me.

Naked, we three embrace the imperatives
Of my hour. An ape's tongue and a hot beak
Take all amalgam fillings from my teeth.

Expressionless, later, those two give me saffron
Light, moult, and six lice for this day's contemplation —
And you, yourself, may sometimes meet us here.

Dying in America

1. The Reserve Pilot

On the billboards
Of my youth, race
Car drivers stared
At their Viceroys;
I, too, was tightly
Packed, often inhaled,
For those things spoke

My name. Later,
After the headlong
Drive down-court,
In parked automobiles
While pom-pom girls
Tongued my navel,
I lighted a Kool.

In our war I flew
And Zippo lighters
Burned even the oxygen
From our briefing rooms
Until, like napalm blooming
Skyward through the overcast,
Peace came, our shut-off engine . . .

II.

Each month thereafter
I flew wing on a peace-
Time colonel: we climbed
Through clouds from Moffit Field
Held for a vector at twenty-nine
On top in the moon-bright dazzle
Beyond our outer marker,

Until to contemplate
That vision I unsnapped the mask
To light my last
Marlboro. My oxygen
Caught fire, took my eyes,

My throat, the flesh
From my ungloved hand;

Pawing to eject
I became the flames
And cockpit metal
Burning through cumulus,
Dying toward earth
Then dead through the roofs
Of two apartment buildings.

Released at last
From almost all illusion
My torso, six teeth,
And my wallet became
Exhibits for the Board Inquiry
Which noted early throat burns
But no known pilot errors.

2. *The Fat Girl*:

At first in our camp things
Were professionally cheerful,
But all through the night
I remembered the highway running
North from our nice apartment
To this clearing in the woods.

At dawn on our second day
We made a "Pile of Flesh"
Then linked our fat arms
To sing the "Calorie Contract" song;
In rows before our unnaturally
Slender counselors, we pledged honor,
But from his cookhouse steps
The owner stared at my thighs.

Bereft, for one week I dreamed
Starlet billboards and the happy
Surgeon, my father, and date-nut bread.
When creek stones cut my feet

I bled, stained our pool, wept;
Each day, I did their Nature-Walk.
Each week at "Saturday weigh-in,"

First, always, to the verified losers,
The owner bellowed out our mail:
From Mother, a slender card from Europe;

From the happy Surgeon, one BOOK
With all the center leaves cut out
By his own scalpels, then filled
With chocolates, "Just to get me by . . ."
Headlong I ran through these woods
Hid behind an oak, and pigged them all.

At summer's end at last we sing
The final break-up of our camp:
Slender before bonfires the big losers
Claim one, complete, new wardrobe;
All others think next year they will return —
Save me — lighter then by twelve whole pounds.

Alone inside my nylon tent
I foresee the highway and our apartment
Where with its frost-breath rising
Our refrigerator waits: where the milk
Is, and — oh — piled-up pecan ice-
Cream, and the shame of chocolate topping.

Yet I have learned my hoarse unlovely
Fat forever shall be both my mace
And their revenge. Once more at home
Again I will devour our suburb-platter
Stretched like a pizza bubbling to the sea.
Against that time each gnawing day of summer
I held back barbiturates, now gorge them all,
    and sleep . . . .

Song: Sunday up the River

When the crocus sights the spring
Its yellow cup to warmth raising
And the martin's purple wing
Slips the wind by feathers singing,
Then we shall lie on this green grass all day
Stroking, oh lightly, our stringed holiday.

Yet this spring consorts with snow
Its vagrant warmth came from below
And the tiger lily snaps its bee,
Gone stamen and bloom, the pod's misery.
And we shall be under this used grass all day
Crying, oh darkly, that winter away.

So drink this up-tipped yellow glass
Lips parted drink purple, drink off this day:
Spread now your long gold hair on this grass
Speak sunshine, oh brightly, by your tongue's disarray.

III.

Patrols

The Frisian Wife

Welcome her lover to the Frisian wife
When ship is at anchor; the sailor home;
Her own food-giver, contriving this life.
Wash the wave-stained garments alone,
Give him upon waking the clean raiment. The shore
Is sweet when thoughts are by love
Restrained, and woman should wait the more
For her man, nor shame him; and above
All be not reeling, but steadfast, nor
Woo the horseback man, when her lord is away.
Often the sea keeps the sailor long, therefore
He sights only the sea's old dismay
Containing the wind that shall not speed.
But the day comes when he steers to the land
Alive and warm and taut with his old need —
Or deep sea holds him, with clutching hand.

(from *The Exeter Gnomes,* adaptation from Old English)

The Knight

Steel encased, the knight rides
Out into the busy world.
It's all out there:
The day and the valley,
Foe, friend, the meal in the hall;
And the maid, the wood, the month of May —
Yes, and the Holy Grail
And in all the streets
In a thousand ways, God shows himself.

Yet, also inside the armor of the knight,
Inside those sinister rings,
Death squats, musing and brooding:
When will the sword, that strange
Liberating blade, spring
Over the iron hedge
To release *me* from this place
That has cramped me many a day
So that I can stretch myself
    And play —
        And sing.

(translated from the German of Rilke: *Das Buch der Bilder*)

Dragon

I.

Our fight was more than fair
The day I — Volant — descried
The knight's lance-tip in sunlight

Advancing at me on the plain;
Being at hunt, for food,
I had no real obligation

To dip my wing's hot shadow
And arouse the horse
And knight to honest combat.

I say, "more than fair"
For each claimed advantage
Of his natural element:

The knight elected earth,
And armor; but I, Volant, I
Was somewhat quicker in the air.

His first charge failed,
And then my kill was clean;
Being at hunt, I stripped

The meat from horse and man
And with the armor on my back
Flew — not hungry — to my lair.

II.

Life, itself, of course went on
And in my turn I judged
Our youth in trials of abstinence

High in the Hartz Mountains
Among our customary barrows;
There I saw my own son

Take vows to guard forever
Our glittering gold hoards
From night attacks by serpents.

Meanwhile, in the way of old mementos
His lance and armor rusted in my cave —
In short, I thought no more about it.

III.

Now, honored among barrows,
Burned haystacks all behind me,
Their scops at song in every abbey

Chimney corner tell their nuns I lost:
Yes, say I, Volant, lost that day
To "virtue" and to the knight's renunciation.

True, the thing took place long ago
Yet I still believe our fight was fair:
I broke lance and horse, and took the meat.

Beyond those facts, I see no conclusion
Except I say that day real virtue
Died. And the Seven Easy Sins took over.

Moby Jane

I.

Legend and rumors at sea
Told Moby Dick of Ahab's
Bright unconditional lance
And of the *Pequod*'s holy fires;

His goal was always Truth
And so, to gather evidence,
He swam from our beds of kelp
And the new calf at my dugs.

Each night for one month
He spied upon the *Pequod*'s decks
Yet saw only unnatural acts,
Obsession, an old man going mad;

Rightly he judged those things
Trivial, or merely secondary
To the *Realpolitik* of headlands,
Or the comprehensive depths of the sea.

II.

On the third day, only to resolve
That morbid chase, he turned back
And stove the *Pequod*, yet left
One man afloat to tell their story;

For years, at home, the old harpoons
Rusted his innocent, white flanks,
But some say Ahab's steel also touched
His mind: now full of ambergris
He calculated order in flotsam,
In dreams, saw all-white continents —
And yet, there was no real malice in him.

The glass fell in the solstice of his years:
In winter he forged to the north, half-blind
By the storm's dark sea-heave spumes —
And grounded off Kodiak. From that reef

All night he preached One World and Love
To sea lions at rut and also unaware
Of men with clubs, at hunt for pelts,
Waiting for dawn to break on that barking shore.

Love's Terrain

Come now to this stylobate country
Underground, this place first I found
At nightfall when an owl's shadow
Whistled across the waist-deep wheat
And I fell end-over-end through a hole in summer

Where ground mist parts, we walk
Beneath two carved limestone idols
Astride this limestone cavern's mouth.
There man-tall sandals rest on the heads
Of animals, all swords unsheathed to guard

These low reverberating corridors.
Here, hanging in rows on hooks like fowl
Or murderous sides of beef, all my past
Falsehoods beg for teeth, cry out
To be eaten in this callow, circumstantial light.

With almost no remorse I contemplate the helmet
Of bronze, its ox teeth yellow, luminous
Among straps broken and urns all in a row
For these things contain my old betrayals:
These artifacts breathe, speak my name.

At the cliff's edge our path ends.
In the dark below dark waters flood
The stones; as we stare this pool
Becomes a rising, blue, undinal eye:
The iris opens and silently we dive therein

Go down, down through the receding hum
Of kelp, wide-eyed, bereft, past
Outcrops where lichens fear to grow
Until at last, we swim upward,
Lie not cleansed on this most hidden ledge.

On this ledge, beyond the solace
Of water, among the stalactites of my years
We discover only the mercy of granite, a lantern
Filled with snow, a fissure's awful reconciliation.
These things I show you honestly before we kiss.

Mandelstam Goes East

Unable or unwilling to support the regime (Stalin), the poet was sent by a friend to the site of a hydro-electric dam under construction, this being an opportunity to celebrate the State.

Bio-Note (undated)

This gorge, the high jumble
Of scaffolds, a fog at noon
Rains down like a waterfall:
The humped backs of six thousand men
Haul buckets of concrete up the ramps
Of policy.

As Mandelstam stares aloft
The sun pulls back the mists,
Reveals a poured, demonic forehead
A terrible idol: those ramps are teeth;
The sullen cable's shriek no voice;
The bucket-men feed only its mouth.
"Ah yes," he says, but knows he will not write.

Trakl, at War

> *A pharmacist on the Polish front, Trakl was detailed to watch helplessly over scores of fatally wounded soldiers. After an attempt to shoot himself failed, the poet was declared a mental case and later, in Cracow, killed himself by taking an overdose of narcotics.*
>
> Anthology, "Note"

Here the moon of Galicia
Falls through the long ward
Windows and turns the corpse-beds
To silver. The hunchbacked,
Silent shadow of an orderly moves
Along the wall, stops, then listens
Intently as the throat of a wound
Coughs, then dies beneath its bandage.

Beyond my ward all fields
Are stubble, and lichens bleed
Beneath the surface of a pond;
A landscape bandaged only by a dark wind.
Beneath an iron bridge at the village edge
The blotched swollen corpse of the boy
Railway worker turns face up in the moonlight
But — not seen — stammers on in the undertow.

Against these catastrophes our Front
Gives way. All sandbag parapets come down.
From our cities the awful siege guns
Of policy uproot the ash tree and wolf's
Den alike in these contaminated woods.
Surgeons, your sutures do not hold
This hoarse retreat. While the dusk grins
I eat blue lakes, and a blue, indifferent sky.

Memorial Day: 1959

I.

When the long iron boat spat us kicking
On the beach near Mers El Kebir
The sea birds twittered past our let-down
Ramp and we ran laughing at a continent,
Not one truly thinking he could die.
But now I think of Elwood Matson
Surprised that night in his own bivouac
Hole, tent poles and his own Garrand
Gouged through his blanket and his blond head,
For a tank track foraged through the lost
Field of his sleep.

II.

And A. C. Roten: often he danced
On our tent ropes and would sometimes sing
Those low, cold Tunisian stars to sleep.
Married, a picture of small girls hiding
In his wallet, and lucky at reconnaissance,
I did not think that he could ever be
Only some rags at Senid Station, thighs severed,
His throat screaming for its mother . . .
And later Graysted, Kibby, Ethred, and Sidney Hines
Died also by S-mines in the Riviera's green
Unforgiving afternoon.

III.

Much later winter came on us near Hagenau
And the season's old revenge of snow shook
The black intricate trees like thunder.
Beaton, and his patrol, in parkas white as breath
Vanished into those mumbling, low-hung boughs.
Later we found them in a shallow bowl
Of that forest, swaying, trussed in the wind,
Flanks maimed, their heads drowned in the terrible snow.
After that we took no prisoners, fought much
Among ourselves with knives, became beasts,
But still, alive.

IV.

Now is this longest day of May again
And while the shrapnel rain rattles this window pane,
I thought to write some formal thing
To say how those alive — being so — see on ahead,
And thought that way to justify their deaths.
But oh when I saw them all once more, again,
I thought: write no lies to those who really died.
Instead let stand this hasty parapet of verse:
For A. C. Roten, Ethred, Matson, Kibby, Graysted,
Paul Sommers, Sindey Hines, John Halstead, and one patrol,
For they are dead.

On Pay Day Night

Picture a desert and the *Panzer* man
Goggled even in death by his own
Sun glasses, obeying a last command

To hold a mortar pit though his roofless
Head sucked sand as our platoon
Aware then only a little of a careless

Sirocco, wondered why — so soon —
Our replacements joined us. But this
Is scarcely remembered for the loom

Of memory creaks and our old tricks,
Such as those grenades of phosphorus
Tossed scalding into bunkers near Bitche,

Fade nicely; by now it was not us
At all for, like juries, can a platoon
Remember? Happy we are that the rust

Hulk sinks, that Victory is a room
Of some weather station where the godless
Anemometer whines, spinning its doom

By consort with storms. Now, careless
Of policy, we froth this bar with our
Spigot laughter and in darkness caress

The purple flesh of conscience for we are
Old He Ones, so heads I win
A pack of Chesters — and we know The Saar

Is no damned good. Now our gin
And tonics roar at closing time,
But we do not forget the day in

Basic we donned Europe's head, bowed
Into our gas masks and took that gas
Which trained us; saw in a mirror how

Our heads were not bird or fish, or brass
Of Idols, that wagging tube no tongue
To speak, nor beak to shatter glass

For here the goggle, head, and mask were one,
Faceless, no sting, no tear, no sound nor laughter;
We clawed, came out like reptiles — not wise, not young.

Wine of Algeria: 1942

One German held the vats of that cold-walled
Winery but he left before our half-track
With antennae and three guns waving crawled
Among the orange trees by the wall in back

And parked concealed. Inside we bought a demijohn;
Five gallons for the three of us.
Understood enough to know the Germans
Drank little but saluted much, took pulp

Seeds, wine, and by distillation made
Fuel from the grapes and by this chemistry
Mounted Stukas from the desert into the sun to raid
The parapets of our artillery.

Next day a woman stared down from her
Window, saw our bodies and our fire.
By noon someone awoke, and we cut our
Trembling fingers on our ration tins.

Finally we left to search more fields
For our Headquarters and while we cursed
Felt the vineyard and the orange groves reel.
Stopped then. Puked all of this back upon their earth.

IV.

Transport To Winter

Aloft the Hang Glider Meditates

Chinstrap and helmet buckled
Against the wind rising from the cliff's
Old antagonism with the sea,

I am my own shadow one thousand
Feet below, a bat-black thing
Running the mist, the shore's spume.

Falling, forever falling through
The up-drafts of this wind's
Mindless, circumstantial weave,

I see the blue, indifferent line
Of all horizons; the sun aloft
And a cormorant's pursuing wings.

I trust the guile of my altimeter,
A wing's pterodactyl memory, a strut's
Weld: these things only hold me.

But the wind dies on an undefended shore,
And being of the sun, of cliff, of the wind,
I go down also to a dark compromise with sand.

Looking at the Sea

Off land's end these working
Fishermen harrow a bay without winds,
A mirror shattered by the sun:
In a row along the lee rail
They follow the wink of lures

Or the gill net's easy
Drift through the fields of kelp
Until the used, vast night descends
And the wheelsman steers them
Toward the hull-down whisper of white buildings.

II.

Athwart a sixteen-fathom reef
This lightship — or coastwise tanker —
Now points shoreward, bridgewing
And keelson wrecked on this shoal,
Deadlights unblinking, still.

Going slowly past the forecastle's
Door, indifferent to their helmsman's
Course marked by the solidarity of all rust,
We see only our own wetsuit-shadows
Adrift among a fallen dialogue of spars.

III.

From this headland's indifferent
Hibernation, look now to the reach
By Steamer Lane where a surfer's
Board glistens orange against the sun,
And wind numbs a sea bird's cry,

There see the water rise,
And going skyward becomes the comber's
Spume, breaks on the ruined bulwark
Of this beach. See flotsam, the hallucination
Of foam, and the surfer — done — on the sunstruck sand.

Hand Tools

Inside this square metal box
Not even a small fire burns
To warm my faithful tools

Auger, Jackplane, Nailset, Bevel;

Numb, with more patience than wood,
Gouged by inexperience — and show it
Extensions only of my own hands and errors

Drawknife, Hammer, Handsaw, Adz.

All through the night their dreams
Are dreams only of tools
Among clouds, forever making other tools

Rasp, Tee Square, Chalkline, Awl;

Yet sunup to them is only the lid lifted
Of one more workday, mostly out of plumb,
And me — sullen — and at least half thumbs

Plumbbob, Mitre, Spokesshave, Level.

Yet beyond the confession of all windows
We whistle the dry curl of cedar shavings
Or caulk the tremors of this, our house:

Auger, Jackplane, Nailset, Bevel;
Drawknife, Hammer, Handsaw, Adz.
Rasp, Tee Square, Chalkline, Awl;
Plumbbob, Mitre, Spokesshave, Level.

The Backhoe

Being made of neither flesh nor feathers
  Nor any life beyond
Diesel fuel ignited only for an instant,
  I stand through the night

Astride this ditch of my own digging.
  Now shorebirds sleep
And the river fog rolls like an old dog
  In off-street kennel parking lots;

All night the night-mortician waits,
  Drinks coffee beside his corpse;
In the blackjack silence of all your streets
  A cat moves grey like stolen goods.

Being not wholly of earth or pipes or water
  I read the implication of debris
Especially when a cannonade of rain
  Sends even the state inspectors

Running to their white construction shacks
  Where deals are made and money
Is the tongue hammering inside their hard hats.
  Then comes a shutdown, sunshine

Holiday: back along my open, morbid trench
  I see only the accommodation of silt
Yet know dirt dug out is only dirt put back come Monday,
  It's only right, and plan enough for me.

Transmigrations

Once I was the heart of a chicken:
The silly one running for a black
Beetle which was innocently crossing

A country road, and for that want
Of judgment now stand all day —
Became a Shikepoke — gazing

Into the surface of this pond
My shadow beating on the green algae,
Its shape much like a chicken's heart.

Before that I was their pet goose,
My feet nailed to a cruel board,
Force-fed for Christmas on table scraps,

Yet not prepared for the morning
Sunlight caught on a raised axeblade,
Their children gathered to see my feathers

And blood spurt into the Christmas wind.
Whereupon without intent I became a dove
Standing white on an ornate dovecote

My past gluttony and a rancid liver
Transposed to tear-shaped, innocent
Songs of peace, for such was my nature.

II.

And yes, I do confess a sameness
To it: the boredom of two legs,
The irrelevance of feathers;

Worse, a beak's headlong imperative
Is like sunlight on a raised axeblade
Seen too late by some astonished worm.

III.

To end these ancient cycles of blood
All birds wish now to become forever
Splendid mirrors in the shape of hearts:

Beveled, framed absolutely of gold,
Each surface true, nailed upright
On the sunstruck wall of a bedroom

There truly to reflect each afternoon
A woman and a man forever undressing
Their bodies a plum-tree branch swaying
Potent, dancing, or at song between sheets.

Orphans: Under Siege

Home was a leaf
Falling in the blue wind
When our mother died.

The leaf became a corridor
Where beehives buzzed
Beyond the wrecked hedge

Where our father also died.
Those things I considered
Even as my bandage wept.

Yet those things passed
And I awoke breathing
A forest, which is this office.

Here the blue leaves
Fell into the corridor-
Fast copier of my mind

And I typed those things
Which in the typing made me :
Low-tar, Cheese Bits, Chicanos;

The ooze of dividends,
The class actions of sorrow.
Those good lies are my joy.

As for my brother,
At dusk always he is
Tilted beside some highway sign;

Later, inside the bedroll
Of his culvert nights
He breathes a forest of whispers;

Or, adrift in the diaspora of off-ramp
Dreams, he becomes forever
A blue leaf running in our blue wind.

Bereavements

In the rim of smoke
Above their poker
Table or beyond a fairway
Marker, when I miss them
So, for one moment,
Silently, I show myself.

Or in a classroom
Where the new woman
Hired to replace me
Lectures, when I miss them
So, for one moment,
Silently, I show myself;

But most often at home
When our five children
Talk or are all reading
Together, Oh, I miss them
So, and for one moment,
Silently, I show myself.

These and also others
I pass on my old feet;
Or with my old hands touch
Their faces for I miss them
So, and in that way,
Silently, I show myself.

Yet I know my skin
Of smoke and transparent
Voice in fact must signify
That I may not betray myself
For neither by shadow nor my footprint
Leave their mark on the passing snow;

Precisely then I know again
Each one I loved now fears
This terrible void without horizons
Which has become my forehead;
Therefore, always, they go onward
Silently past or even through me,
Who miss them so,
And yet, here, would show myself.

Elegy: My Own

Come morning
The small ashes
Of this burned-out year
Settle at last
On the get-well
Cards; between sheets,
Gradually, I cool
In the degreeless
Hope of this day's sun.

Suspended so,
A carp floating
Mindless in the last
Talons of winter ice,
I would hear the topography
Of renewal, would view the off-shore
Soundings of this confirmed
Yet circumstantial voyage.

II.

At noon
Only the stipulations
Of known things abide
In my dressertop's unwavering
Light: three keys, my wallet,
My own photograph, in uniform,
Age twenty-six, the frame, oak.

Now their stretcher
Sneaks in on solid wheels
Of rubber. Our children
Hold open all the doors.
Beside the curb a man
Buckles the white straps,
Thinks mostly about tonight.

III.

At a river's bridge
The tugboat horn
Floats me among shoe factories:
I wish to make alive again
The Lucas boy, my friend,
Who jumped from the beam
Of his father's barn
Through a hayfork
Not half concealed;
Someway I wish
To return those sun glasses
I pillaged from the locker
Of the bombardier
Whose Mitchell bomber snuffed
In flame into the Mediterranean.

IV.

Neither discovery
Nor underwater, iron
Hulks are now at issue.
I have become the sum
Of remembered, curious, choices past:
Of ash, of ice, the adept
Leverage of wallets;
A mirror's unrequited adoration,
Children opening the doors.

Surely *this* voice is my own voice
Now a voice of ash within a temperate
Urn, a voice poised yet well at roost,
Possessed by these dark, roosting fowl
All in a row in a row of dying trees
On this rapacious shore. My voice
Vacant, yet listening for the storm to come.

If I Should Die . . .

Think Then of Earth:

Concealed beneath get-well
Cards, the paid-for grief
Of floral tributes, the lacquered
Piety of limousines, or a mortician's
Trained, paradisial gaze, I see

Well the duplicities of clay.
By definition common, all dirt
At night seeks the level of water,
Warms to a mole's devious intent,
In April grows wort, rot, erosion.

Yet, against the brute
Convenience of soil, the cumulative
Richness of old men's graves,
When I arise singing to light
Who then shall wish to own his lot?

So Consider This:

Inside a clear, large
Jar of clearest, tempered glass
Shaped as a man at ease
About my size is shaped,
By two handles and two ropes

Hang me among wisteria
Entombed in a golden jar of honey.
Sealed strong with wax, swaying,
At my feet fruit in a blue bowl,
Each day changed by the changing sun

This is more civilized than sleep
By clay. And, being also mindless,
Ten million bees cannot object. Nor am
I morbid, dear, for in this death,
As in life, I do not wish to leave you.

Lay Down These Things

1. *In the Morning:*

Sales goals, the personal challenge,
Quota by load-factor, or contact
Hours, eggs over, six-lane traffic lights;

Be done also with target mailing
For bereavement, witchcraft in cities,
Tycoons, the black holes of legislation.

These things lay down beside a lunch
Of Oilers, Vikings, Giants, Rams,
Wide receivers of the bottom line.

2. *Past Noon:*

Coast Guard parades, architectural
Competitions, house-pet mortuaries,
The Pentagon's most secret pension plans;

Be done also with conference calls,
Love slaves, tums, the color consultant,
Poets teaching mostly for the money.

These things lay down beside roomettes,
Turbo-sex with chilled white wine. . .
These things, these things lay down.

3. *After the Evening News:*

Cat food odors, the old woman dead
On the stairs, her face covered with a towel,
Romance, sister cities, Associates of Kissinger.

Be done also with the new surgeon's
Blood-addiction for in my time I seek dark
Ground, honestly cleared, my place to die:

Fighting in old age for my country,
Love, mischance, or motorcycle racing,
Not brave, but something like a man.

V.

Adventures In Narration

Spoor

I. Dog

I say there's cruelty
Beneath tolerance and I say affection
Is the shoe that kicks your ribs

But to tell the truth I run
Beneath my clothesline of necessity
And thus avoid their grocery trips:

They park me with the car
Then bring back meat in paper sacks
Easy to rip — but always out of reach.

And I say there's cruelty
In those cans of "doggie" food
They fetch to me: suet and liver

Warmed but not quivering
Like good live meat tracked
Then killed by my own illicit teeth.

Oh, past nightfall I patrol
Their shrubs and can pretend
To guard their eunuch flower beds,

And I've known some foolish dogs
Who yelped in fields beneath the moon,
But I would not advise it.

Why, I know six bitch dogs
Within one hot mile of here
All easy to mount, and all spayed.

Still you have to live some way
So I have learned to lick a hand:
It's expected, and helps avoid the pound.

I say if dogs had hands for paws
We'd soon see who barked in pens
Near laboratories — evolution notwithstanding.

As for facts, I know my vet is fast
(He's only in it for the money)
So a dog's life is that, and nothing more.

Meanwhile my creed is this: Defile
Their roses every chance and live
To kill the Persian cat which sleeps next door:
A dog's life is only that, and nothing more.

II: Cat

Why should I stir from my warm place
For all the world outside? I like silk,
And our rug with tufts of white is grace

Enough for me. What's more, my milk's
Homogenized and my basket's always clean;
It's true I simply will not sleep on quilts

And it's been years since any raucous, obscene
Fleas shuttled through my well-combed fur.
You see, I'm certain things are what they seem

And so I smile and watch that little cur
Across the street — yes, smile — for *it* barks,
Defiles their roses, growls at food, is vulgar

Beyond belief. I say my own remarks
Confirm good breeding and of course
I do have papers. I say my thought marks

Well a sensual, Persian mind which the hoarse
Paws of Airedales shall not put down. It's right
That I should live forever, *sans* remorse:

Give us our fish in our clean dish
Make ladies whisper, when we're asleep
Give us our basket, give us dry heat
Forgive us the dust which corrupts our feet.

Oh, as for children
I've heard
They're a lady's delight,

But not — please —
By a Tom
Under shrubbery at night.

III: Coyote

The night
Stalks from these foothills
Mouth-dark and more silent
Than any cougar

But I
Am scabbed by ticks, my guts
Burn in the night-thirst of rabies
And so, alone,

I die
Beyond my pack's old authority.
Yet once they harried the landscape
At my back

And I
Led them down the neon throat
Of suburbs and saw my shadow leap
Like a scythe blade

Over fences.
There we ate filth from garbage cans
And broke the backs of Airedales
Where they whined.

Now I
See rabid visions of the night,
See certain, new, unleashed authority
To be seized by cunning.

Oh on
That day I shall command these hills
To convulse, to send out packs not yet dreamed
By grocery shoppers;

I shall
Lope howling down the overwhelming
Sky and shall upheave the pipes of sewers
From their graves.

That day
I shall be sleek as a tank car
Followed by the bitch pack running,
Each one in heat;

That day
No child or wheel-chair cripple
Shall escape this Joy you now see in me.
Until then, wait.

Jack and Jill

1. Of Jack:

The hill, that pail of water,
My legs, suddenly kicking the sky,
Then going down stones in grass
I tore my arm's flesh, became fable.

When young I was not good
At water, feared stallions, despised
Sheep, was sly among stanchions,
Slept at noon in their haymow's hay.

Largely to avoid the dray-horse
Laughter of older hands at table
And my aunt's mending-needle tongue,
I went through a hedge to the highway

Arrived by freight truck in your city.
Here I neither starved nor wept,
At once found work in *Sid's All Nite*
ACE CAFE, often had my ass pinched

By Sid's always half-drunk wife.
Soon I shot their 8-ball, rotation,
Or billiards for the house, am quick
To rack, wear pink, am called *The Stick*.

That hill, the pail, a so-called
Broken crown is now not remembered
And my thought is this: hustle the
Marks, chalk well, avoid the long shot

Down the rail. And as for money,
I know the true-stroked ball rolls
True, and Brother, I say if you
Play long enough with me, you lose.

2. Of Jill:

Always they say "Tumbling
After," a girl in innocence
Confirming yet another fall

Caused, it's said, by apples.
But I was there and know
The facts: too proud for work,

Ever clumsy, he merely slipped
On cowshit, feigned his injury,
Bruised only his jacket sleeve.

Oh, I laughed, then filled
Our pail, easily carried it down,
Found him wet, bawling among blue

Straw flowers in the late
Summer of my error for being moved,
I took pity, kissed him well.

Error, for at my touch Jack
Fled through a hole in the hedge . . .
And, if asked, I might have followed.

Came fall, came the dispensation
Of winter. Each day through March
I felt embraced by white, wet,

Sheets of snow, yet slept stormy
Beneath eaves, did mending for the aunt,
Dreamed summer, dreamed new-mown

Hay, was fearful even in dreams
To lay or not to lay beside him
When he showed me plain his sex

Curved, not small, white,
Illuminated in a slant of light
From the roof — and most engaging.

Came spring's promise of forsythia,
And soon the cold regret of my bed
Passed, as a failed crop passes,

Or near bedtime, as an outside
Hound snuffles once at memory's door . . .
Yet, if asked, I might have followed.

Being plain, being good at water,
Now not much bereft among their barns,
I see Jack plain, most clearly.

Clumsy always, too fond of colors,
Drawn to himself, to exhibition,
What he would have most was admiration.

Being now much more the woman,
I use Jack's not so easy lesson,
And know one thing most privately:

Come fall I will have — and soon —
To bed that good-boned, hack-mouthed,
Fair-skinned son of their best farrier

And should he plainly wish it so,
Beneath my eave we will trim a hoof,
Fit the shoe once before the nailing.

Our Masters, Revisited;

Something like Dryden

Where I walked one day
Into the hills upland
From Santa Cruz

I saw a green arroyo,
Both path and passage,
Leading me aloft

Into an azure field
Where — not as lights
Precisely — yet not shades

Three writers of our past
Rose from their work,
Said, "Do stop here."

Faulkner, taller now,
More joyful than
I remembered, spoke:

"That time in Oregon,
We talked half the night,
At dawn viewed the ocean;

Now we meet again
And because we judge
Your talent fair, we . . ."

"Wish to hear from you,"
And Dreiser made their point:
"How is it with our literature?"

"Not excluding the paradigm
Of our poetry," for so
Wallace Stevens spoke.

At first, astonished,
I replied, — Tell me,
Are you here each day?

"Here we have good desks;
And, correctly, this place
Has no walls, is panoramic."

"That's because we wrote too much."
— Do lesser talents also work here?
"Not exactly," Dreiser said,

"Only those less driven."
"Or Southerners, less in debt."
"Money," Stevens said, "*was* secondary."

Faulkner shrugged, and we
Watched L _____ and D _____
Pass, their feet four stumbling scabs.

"They 'used' our poetry,
Slandered one another,"
Stevens gravely shook his head;

"So they walk insparable,
Quoting their worst lines."
— And those grinding scabs?

"Some details," Dreiser said,
"Are best withheld," and Faulkner
Saw an unintended irony.

Soon I understood
These three rose each day,
Released save from themselves;

Each day in this lucid
Place they revised forever
Those things they loved best.

"Oh yes, I write
'Sunday Morning'; now
Form is my obsession,"

Wallace Stevens said.
"And me, it's *Carrie*,
And I expect soon to get it right . . ."

"It's not like me, but there are
Fifty versions of my *Bear*."
They smiled, pleased this was so.

Soon it came my turn
To tell our present situation:
The writer's way inside

Our capitalistic system:
Those taken in the scramble
For money, dissolved by drink,

Friends who bartered
Talent for the symphonic
Illusion of drugs, or the honey

Of protest. Others fell
Into a jackal-agent's bed,
Or for quick fame, now,

Became personalities of straw,
Could very well imitate
Themselves, or feed the presses.

"Things change not much,"
The lawyer said, "Our time
Gave yours ample precedent,

And what was really lost
With the death of Bodenheim?
And MacLeish: now alive or dead?"

I did not reply,
Not say for they could not know
Writers now are much alike:

Some write for property,
Some speculate in land;
Some poets revise for tenure,

Fringe benefits aforethought.
Nor do we expect of us the less
In this slow, Golden Age

Of Capitalism — as we know it.
These thoughts I concealed
In deference to their own, unexamined

Ideologies — Stevens not excepted.
Then Faulkner lit his barnyard
Pipe, "Ah tried, all my life,"

And here he broke off speech.
Too late in this fearful place
He still sought resolutions.

Faulkner paused, then wept.
They placed their hands upon
His shoulders, said things not heard

By me. Yet to see them so,
Each in his own isolated way
Rising to unlikely fellowship,

Strangely moved me also to tears,
And as I watched their
Blue shades grew, grew larger

Until beneath the whisper
Of our ancient, burning sun
They disappeared — were gone.

Whereupon I felt more alone
Than ever I remembered,
But said aloud, — Enough, no more.

Slowly I turned back
Along the path and passage
Of a soundless green arroyo.

While that lucid afternoon
Of azure crumbled into dusk
The first scab squirmed inside my foot.

Nightfall, path, the retaliation
Of stones, my shadow walked mute
Beneath an overhang of granite:

Those things I remember,
And when the terrain was again
Familiar, I stopped to rest.

When the Bay bent skyward
To the moon, I felt the dark
Residual wings of this dark world

Which we do ride so brightly down,
Down until that day the books of men
Shall drop us burning from some page.

In the Compounds of Error

(after Saneatsu)

JUDAS:

They are saying I hanged myself?
Well, sit down — have a sherbet. Here,
You take my seat. Of course I'm happy
To tell you everything I ever knew
About Jesus, and I'll give you names
Of gentlemen who will absolutely verify
What I say. They really will.

My little place? This litle garden?
Oh, I like privacy, and speaking
Very, very frankly the lady here
Needs me — ah — to do her rents.
And I need a little leisure
To sit in her garden and someday
Gather opinions, set my record straight.

I see what you're thinking:
My lit-tle fee. Oh, I sensed it.
Of course I took my fee —
No! Never did attempt to hang myself!
Much, *much* less than that . . .
People do exaggerate, you know.
And a fee is not the issue. Right?

For background: say I've slept late
These past six months; her garden
Really is a satisfaction. We eat
Melon at ten, and on nice days
I walk inside these walls,
Do meditation. Gardens somehow speak to me;
Like yourself, I really am intellectual.

Another cup of wine . . . No?
Well, then make a note:
I still love him — I really do —
In most respects. His faults,
And here I'll be absolutely candid,
Were of intellect. When you listened
The words were fine. But what then?

Of all the men near him
(More people left at the end
Than is generally known) I alone
Dealt in issues which were real.
I knew he needed someone like me;
Otherwise, he was too ethereal,
He made all things seem less than real.

You see exactly what I mean?
Good. Now consider just one thing:
Veracity. At first I was taken
By the idea of God's kingdom. But
Was it here, or not? If after death
— A cunning doctrine — then where?
I felt he glossed the point over.

Or, let's make a clear distinction:
He had rhetoric and cunning;
But there are minds — like ours.
He, himself, said it, "Be cunning
As serpents," for cunning (not brains)
Was his strength. This could offend
For I needed forthright answers. You see?

Assuredly, Sir, we see a lit-tle
Vanity in everyone. But he was also
Obstinate and would not recognize
Wisdom in others. One good case is
The Pharisees. They might have helped,
But he rolled his eyes upward, said,
"Oh ye of little faith." His mace,

His crutch. For what it's worth
That phrase could well become your epigraph,
For this was his answer
To all disagreement, as though he
Were a law, himself, against dissent.
"Oh ye of little faith" *was* useful
But just hear, from me, the consequence.

That way he asked only obeisance,
With no thought, no evidence implied.
So fishermen, etc., had only to assent.
Dogmatic he was, but not himself genteel;
So educated minds could despise

Him. All his people were ignorant,
Or criminals, had no feelings of their own.

"Oh ye of little faith." Oh I
Remember it like bells, or a drum pounding.
By that imperative he monopolized
God for himself, and I have examples:
In the wilderness. And also he said
Salvation came only if he, himself,
Were — in his own illogical way — respected.

Now quote me on this accurately:
"When he took this God for himself,
Judas gradually decided to withdraw."
Yes "gradually" . . . to avoid embarrassments.
My fee was really only a symbol.
Moreover, Jesus said he, alone,
Was God. That way he kept his flatterers.

Would you read back that one?
Now, I'll state something else:
"Judas saw the hard side;
Namely, knew the work could not succeed."
His people were dirty, and I for one
Was embarrassed to work with them,
Though the poor sometimes were too good.

Often at night beside a wall
Or in some corner near a garden
Our meetings brought out a feeling
In me that anyone would remember
With affection. And I do remember.
I have no hatred, oh, not really;
They merely lacked power, and were not wise.

Plans? Well, you can state this:
First, I'll lay aside some money,
And then call some right-thinking people;
I'll show that two can play his game,
But I'll reform the world. I mean
The real reforms of land, of tax, of rents.
So write nothing until you hear more. From me.

JOHN:

All night I write
Letters and toward dawn
Our messengers depart.
I drink a horn of water
But these days eat not much.

And seldom sleep.
You say you want the facts?
And Judas says all those things?
Well, stand here. I'm busy
And have nothing at all to feed you.

Hate Judas? Me?
Oh, I think not,
But I have always known he seeks
Merely justice and order and that's
A defect central to his character.

The worthy rejoice
In the dunnage of God's
Love, but Judas evades complicity.
He compares his rents, his income, with those
Who hold more property than his woman;

So Judas feels
Not paid enough — by God.
Embroiled thus, Love's other
Kingdoms each day elude the viper
Of his strong, unseemly intellect.

Judas alone
Would say The Master *used*
Women, for His ulterior motives.
Precludes compassion. The Master loved
The purity of women implied by their weeping.

But — I grant —
Your epigraph on "Little
Faith" is apt. I do feel
Precisely that in each cock-crow
Watch of my private, unaltered approbation.

Too little faith:
That's all we had,
And by comparison had none at all
Until the delirium of palm fronds
By Gethsemane seemed to convulse us.

Oh, I confess it,
I will seldom go now
Inside any garden. Yet, daily,
I bear witness that our "Little
Faith" confounds the tackle of our intellect

Until it seems
This room and all those vast
Tactile ministries of the sun
Shall one day be consumed by Faith
Rampant, at last, across this world's wilderness.

His great appeal?
Why, I should say The Master
Exploited practicality, exhumed
From mere rhetoric the felicities
Denied by parchment — and most Pharisees.

It's true, The Master
said He, alone, was God's
Son. Then by example proved
His own conviction, brought the tongues
Of His Father's own cross-weighted love to earth.

Say more? Me?
By way of qualification?
Well, put down that certain Scribes
Are also upright. Say Judas is admirable
In all the little ways we always knew . . .

Even so, the malicious
May become omniscient, and Judas
Yet may fall with his fine wool robes flapping
Into some new, undreamed garden of surrender . . .
Meanwhile, night is here.
Goodbye . . .

Work to do.

Journals from the Ark

I - *Thursday: Third Watch*

Dark now
And even the Hyena sleeps
But our complaint of inadequate straw
Goes not answered by management;
At bottom
Noah's scheme is not believed in
And even the degenerate Sloths
Sway then slobber and attempt speech.

Not soon
Shall we forget our own recruitments:
Ropers unannounced, prophecy of flood,
Quotas, betrayal, and arbitrary pairings;
Or worse,
No consultation with our Elders
So of course certain malcontents
Stepped forward, eager to leave our customary glades.

In pairs,
Hobbled, reviled by those not chosen,
We pressed forward at night acrosss stones
Until, one dawn, we saw this mad contraption,
This ark:
As yet not caulked, no oars, no anchor.
On deck, our Swans hissed in disbelief;
Below, all quarters were identical, and Giraffes wept.

The deadlights
Warped, Ocelots claimed the beams aloft,
And after two nights the sinister
Reptiles rustled in caucus — and no rain.
We give
Noah, and all management, less than a week
Before this ill-constructed cage bursts
Beneath the outrage of tusk, and hoof, and beak.

II - *Evidently Friday: A.M.*

Afloat now
The Rhinos vomit all through the night,

The larger Reptiles refuse bilge-duty,
Our piled-up filth breeds certain mutiny;
        The consensus
Of water-holes, the covenants of our forests
Are gone forever. Instead, lust obtains
And we see unnatural acts, especially with Camels.

        Yet who shall
Forget our first storm's mighty paw:
Plank ends, a man, and all cordage
Harried aloft into the red, night sky;
        'Tween decks
The chaos of leaks set all our stables
Awash, two thwart-beams came down,
And in our High Council all order vanished.

        This enterprise
Itself is still the thing most questioned:
What rational polity can hold an ark
Even remotely superior to governance
        Under law,
The antique imperatives of foothills?
Or off-spring, in season, the Wolf's design?
Here scurvy engenders impotence. We drift.

III - *Position not Known: Calm*

        On deck
Our spies, the rodents, report
Much cargo still adrift, the watch asleep;
The women wail in the lee scuppers.
        And Noah?
That common sheepsherd gone to sea?
Each day he sights green, new "continents,"
Then sulks in the forepeak conniving with "God."

        Here below
We are victims of some monstrous
Ego: this thing ill-planned, clandestine,
Our deaths by drowning already presumed.
        Our High Council,
Therefore, condemns any and all management
For crimes against all species held herein,
The Reptiles, at will, to enforce our resolution.

Our last
Analysis holds this "God" not competent;
Shows willful neglect; is obsessed by loyalty.
So we now conclude long-time famine at sea
Shall bring
A new solidarity among exploited creatures.
Last night even the Reptiles coiled to applaud
A Beasts' Revolt: *Strike Once, Remake the World.*

IV - *Epilogue*

The outcome,
Officially, is now a matter of record:
Our catastrophic ark, leaking to the end,
Creaked once, then past midnight went aground.
Management defected.
Neaped, abandoned, with our hooves
We hammered the rotted timbers
Then, triumphant, we set all creatures free.

And for what?
Only mudflats, the terrain not at all familiar,
No spoor, no policy. Sadly we dispersed,
Walked away more bereft than anyone imagined.
Much later
In our customary glades, nothing had changed.
And — of course — we met herds — the jolly survivors —
The ones who jeered, or because of sloth remained.

Yes, they laughed.
After one week of rain they had removed
Easily to the mountains, and there each day
Looked at the sky, said, "Gents, all floods recede."

As for Noah,
We hear but one persistent, leafy rumor:
Overnight all his women became fecund,
And now that Ark's chaos has become his Law.

By custom,
However, we Elephants always remember.
At ease now, still the sovereigns of our domain,
We reflect at times on that arbitrary voyage.
In candor,
We conclude not much was ever proved:
Noah lives on and on, a sheepsherd forever.
Our Reptiles crushed then ate both traitor doves.

Envoi: A Clutch of Dreams

The forked path in the woods
Dreams of a crossroads, dreams
The perfection of concrete divides
A valley into four equal fields;

The shoat at the slaughterhouse door
Remembers a fine white gate
At the barn-end of a meadow
Where corn calls with the voice of a man.

Waterlogged, an orange life raft
Drifts on the terrible Pacific
Then sinks, still dreaming of atolls,
And another crew roistering ashore.

And I, on this forked path
In dreams see fine white gates,
And I ride this orange-raft world
Downward to coral, where this dream ends.

(photograph by Michael Sykes)

About the Author:

JAMES B. HALL is a distinguished poet, novelist, and short story writer.

Of an Ohio farm background, he attended Miami University (Ohio) briefly and after long-term service overseas in World War II was awarded the B.A., M.A., and Ph.D. in literary history, criticism, and imaginative writing—at the University of Iowa.

Hall brings a wide variety of experience in the world to all his writing. After the farms he was a merchant sailor, worked in canneries and at the liquor trade; drafted in World War II, he was trained for the infantry, and became a Chief Warrant Officer with service from North Africa to Innsbruck. At war's end he was assigned to Military Government detachments and as a waterfront Labor Officer presided over the first waterfront union meeting in Germany. Biographical details are covered in Volume 12, *Contemporary Authors* Autobiographical Series (1990).

A literary artist of unusual range in an age of literary specialization, Hall credits the examples of several distinguished literary mentors: Paul Engle, Hansford Martin, and Andrew Lytle; Robert Lowell and R.P. Warren; Austin Warren and Richard Chase, among others, all in the Humanistic tradition of letters.

In 1946 Jim married Elizabeth Cushman. The couple have five grown children. Over the years Hall has combined a writing career with various university posts, usually of a pioneering kind: a founder of both the *Northwest Review* and the Creative Writing program at Oregon, he was then on the cadre of U.C. Irvine, and later the founding provost of the Arts College (now Porter College) at U.C. Santa Cruz, where the college major focused on aesthetics. For career details see *Who's Who* (current), or similar.

The Regents, University of California, named the James B. Hall Art Gallery (Santa Cruz); Cabrillo College sponsors an annual prize for fiction in his name. The literary papers are at Miami University and available to scholars. Presently Hall is an independent writer and resides in Eugene, Oregon.

COVER DESIGN based on "Five Foxes," an etching by Israhel Van Meckenem, the Younger (born ca. 1450, died 1503). Meckenem sold his engravings to painters, printmakers, and craftsmen—who might then have used the individual foxes printed on sample sheets, as needed.

The text of *BEREAVEMENTS* was set on computer in Adobe Postscript, Palatino 9 on 11 leading. Text editing, book layout, and design are by Judith Shears, Castle Peak Editions.